ARCHAEOLOGY FOR KIDS

AFRICA

TOP ARCHAEOLOGICAL DIG SITES AND DISCOVERIES

GUIDE ON ARCHAEOLOGICAL ARTIFACTS
5TH GRADE SOCIAL STUDIES

BABY PROFESSOR

EDUCATION KIDS

Speedy Publishing LLC

40 E. Main St. #1156

Newark, DE 19711

www.speedypublishing.com

Copyright 2017

In this book, we're going to talk about some of the top archaeological dig sites in Africa. So, let's get right to it!

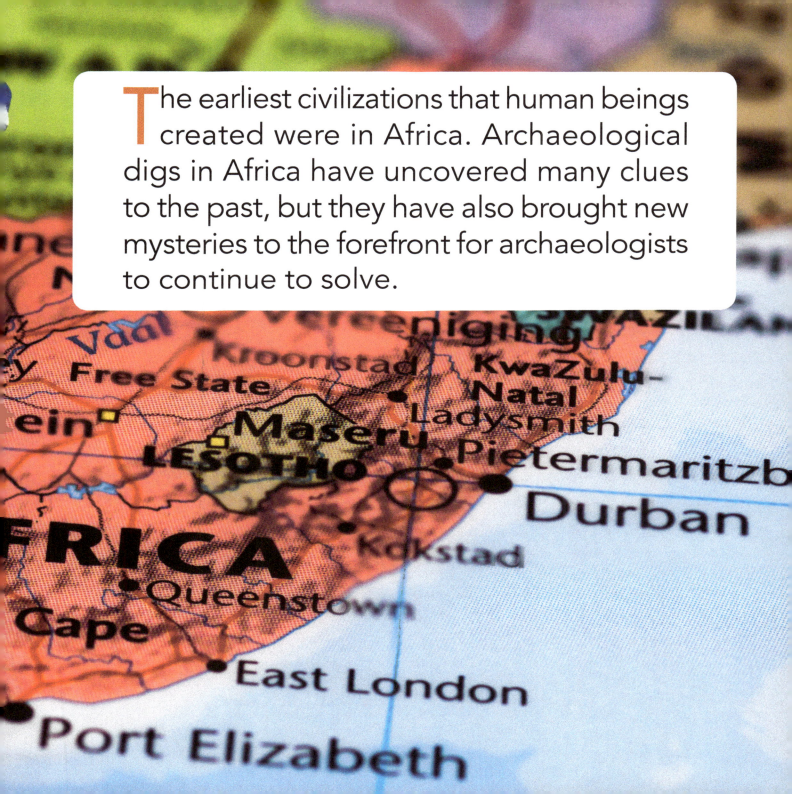

The earliest civilizations that human beings created were in Africa. Archaeological digs in Africa have uncovered many clues to the past, but they have also brought new mysteries to the forefront for archaeologists to continue to solve.

STONE CIRCLES IN THE GAMBIA

THE STONE CIRCLES OF SENEGAL AND GAMBIA

In West Africa, in the country of Senegal and the country of Gambia, there are large stone constructions that date to around 300 BC. People lived there in communities and archaeologists believe that the stone circles may have had religious significance. Human remains have been found, so it's possible that these mysterious stone pillars arranged in circles may have simply been graves where rituals for the dead took place.

Some of the pillars are taller than others, so it's likely that the taller pillars mark the site where an important chieftain was buried. The effort needed to remove these stones from a quarry, transport, and shape them was enormous since there are over 30,000 laterite stones in total at the different sites. The ancient people who did this work must have had a considerable amount of knowledge regarding both geology and how to use tools to shape the iron.

The largest of the sites is located at Sine Ngayene in Senegal. At this site, there is evidence of the stone quarries as well as work with iron smelting. Artifacts layered in the ground show that communities of ancient peoples lived and worshipped there for over 700 years.

MEROE, SUDAN

The ancient city of Meroë has a history dating back to 800 BC. In the Bible, the city is mentioned in the book of Genesis, although it is called Aethiopia.

THE PYRAMID OF MEROE

This ancient city had stone palaces, evidence that displays advanced knowledge of iron work, and distinctive-looking pyramids. The people who lived there had an advanced culture from the Egyptians and the surrounding areas had fertile soil as well as large deposits of iron, which was valuable for the creation of tools and weapons.

As a result, Meroë became a very important trade location and traders came to buy and sell from as far away as the civilizations of Rome, Persia, and Greece. In addition to its trade with these countries, the city also traded with some of the earliest explorers from China and India. The citizens of Meroë even raised and exported elephants for the armies of foreign countries.

MOTHER AND BABY ELEPHANT

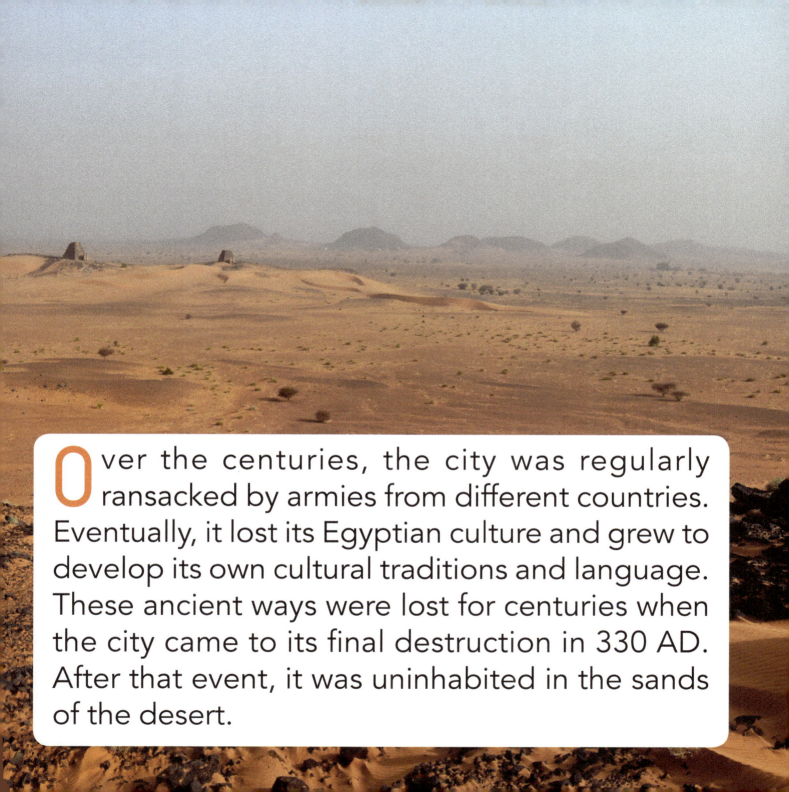

Over the centuries, the city was regularly ransacked by armies from different countries. Eventually, it lost its Egyptian culture and grew to develop its own cultural traditions and language. These ancient ways were lost for centuries when the city came to its final destruction in 330 AD. After that event, it was uninhabited in the sands of the desert.

There, in 1821, archaeologists began to excavate the 200 pyramids of Nubian design that remained as a testament to the people who had lived there. The written language that has been found has never been deciphered and still holds many mysteries about this sophisticated ancient culture.

GREAT ZIMBABWE STONE HOUSES, MASVINGO, ZIMBABWE

The stone houses of Zimbabwe date back almost 1,000 years. The city covers over 18,000 acres and has three compounds of stone construction that were built without any mortar. Archaeologists discovered that the type of masonry used for these sophisticated ancient constructions was different than any other stone work done in the surrounding area. It's believed that the city took over 300 years to complete.

At one time, the complex housed over 15,000 people. Artifacts that have been discovered there, show evidence that the government was a monarchy. The people who lived there practiced religion, had active commerce, and worked with livestock and mining.

GREAT ZIMBABWE

CRUCIBLE

S ome of the ancient artifacts found at the location include many types of glass beads, tools and sites for metalworking, such as grinding stones and crucibles. Crucibles are vessels used for holding materials that must undergo very high heat for melting down metals. Perhaps the most mysterious of the artifacts are eight Egyptian-looking birds that were carved from soapstone.

These 13-inch high sculptures were originally seated on pedestals. The sculptures combined bird and animal features and it's not clear what their original function was. They could have been religious icons or they could have stood for some of the prominent kings. They were discovered in an area called the "Eastern Enclosure," which is situated on a hill and thought to be a location where priests performed religious rituals.

EASTERN ENCLOSURE

WAGONS IN GOLD MINE

It's not yet known with certainty why this ancient civilization declined. Some experts believe that once the resources from Zimbabwe's gold mines were depleted that this may have been the cause of the city being abandoned. At this point in time, only about 2% of the city has been excavated, so future archaeologists have a lot of work to do to uncover more of the secrets of this ancient stone city.

THE LALIBELA CHURCHES, ETHIOPIA

The Lalibela Churches, located in Ethiopia, were constructed in the 1100s as Christianity became popular in Africa. Because of Muslim conquests, Christians couldn't make pilgrimages to the holy land. King Lalibela wanted to find a solution. He commissioned the building of the Lalibela Churches. Africans who became Christians came to this location to pay homage and the site was designed to look like the holy places in Jerusalem.

PORTRAIT OF KING LALIBELA

BASALTIC ROCK STONE

The churches located there weren't constructed from materials that were brought to the site. Amazingly, they are stone monoliths that were carved directly out of existing basalt blocks of rock. Basalt is a type of volcanic rock. The doors, columns, windows, roofs, and floors were carved out of stone. There are also places that have openings that lead to catacombs or secret hermit caves.

The churches are elaborately decorated with icons from the earliest Christian teachings. Bete Giyorgis, which means the Church in honor of Saint George, is considered to be one of the best-preserved religious structures from that time period worldwide.

TOURISTS AT SAINT GEORGE CHURCH

Muslim armies tore down part of the city in the 1500s, but most of the buildings still survived. People still live there today.

BAKONI, SOUTH AFRICA

Located in Mpumalanga in the country of South Africa, the Bakoni Ruins are thought to date back 200,000 years. The ruins located there consist of enormous groups of stone terracing. There are settlements as well as connecting roads. The artifacts and construction ruins point to advanced technology and innovations in agriculture that the ancient people living there were using.

Archaeologists are puzzled and many strange theories have been proposed about the site since the evidence of the technology used there seems very far advanced for its time period.

One of the most important features is a site that is called Adam's Calendar. It is a 30-meter wide stone circle with monoliths carefully positioned within it.

Archaeologists believe that the stone monoliths align with the stars located in the formation known as Orion's Belt. They believe that it's evidence of how these ancient people kept charts of the passing time and seasons.

ORION'S BELT WITH POINTED STARS

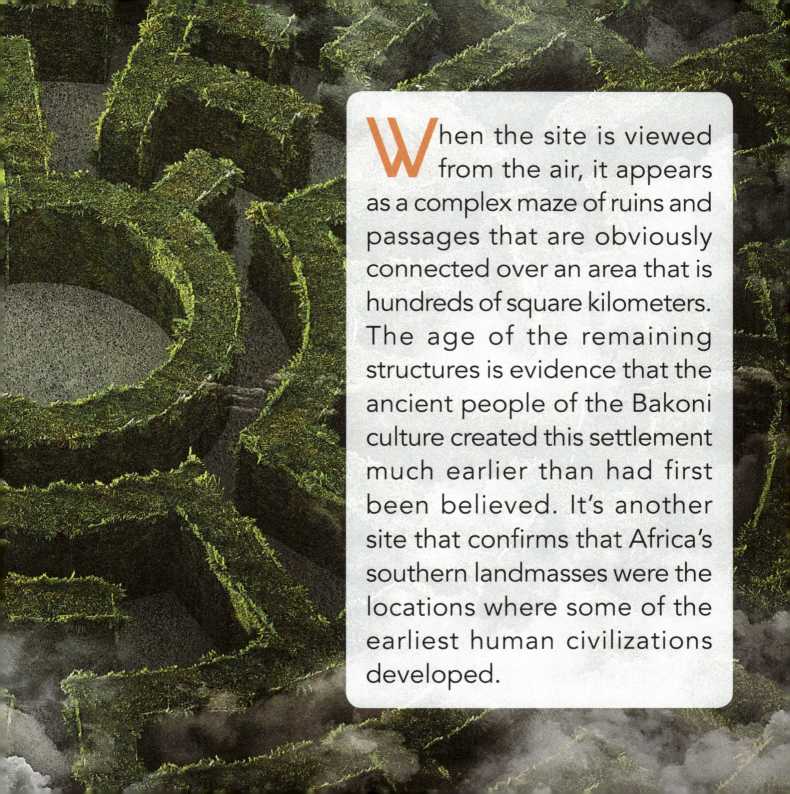

When the site is viewed from the air, it appears as a complex maze of ruins and passages that are obviously connected over an area that is hundreds of square kilometers. The age of the remaining structures is evidence that the ancient people of the Bakoni culture created this settlement much earlier than had first been believed. It's another site that confirms that Africa's southern landmasses were the locations where some of the earliest human civilizations developed.

KING TUT'S TOMB IN EGYPT

The ancient civilization of the Egyptians is filled with amazing archaeological finds. Perhaps the most famous is King Tut's Tomb, which was discovered by Howard Carter in 1922. The tomb is located in a necropolis, called Valley of the Kings, close to the city of Luxor, Egypt.

VALLEY OF THE KINGS

THE ENTRANCE OF THE TUTANKHAMEN'S TOMB

Archaeologists thought they had uncovered most of the treasures that were to be found in this ancient burial site, but Carter did not agree. He thought that the tomb of King Tutankhamun was still somewhere under the desert sands. He searched for over six years and was just about to give up and lose funding to continue the search until he found its entrance under some huts being used by workmen.

The tomb was filled from wall to wall with priceless treasures. There were ornate statues, built-to-scale model boats, life-size chariots, chairs adorned with gold and precious jewels, and the canopic jars, which held King Tut's bodily organs.

PHARAOH TUTANKHAMEN

There was also a gold funeral mask for the young Pharaoh made with 22 pounds of gold and an elaborate sarcophagus with his mummified body.

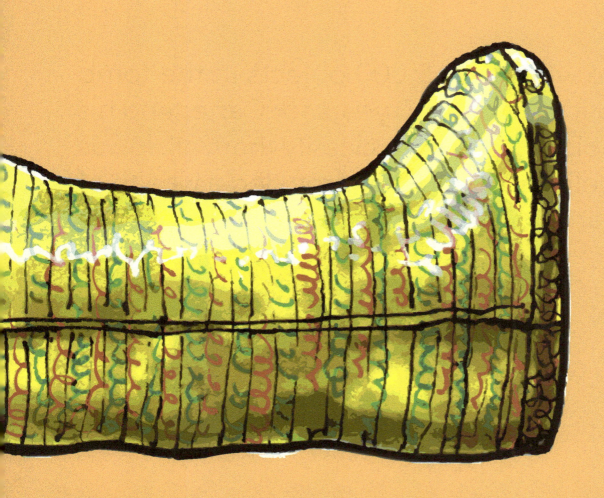

There were over 5,000 objects in the tomb and it took over 10 years for Carter and his archaeological team to classify them all. It was an unbelievable find that provided a wealth of information about the Egyptian culture.

SUMMARY

Some of the most fascinating archaeological finds in the world have been found on the African continent. The earliest human civilizations developed there, and, because of this, Africa has been called the "cradle of human civilization." Stone circles, giant pyramids constructed from stone, stone churches, and hidden tombs with priceless treasures are evidence of the religious and cultural behavior of the people of Africa's ancient civilizations.

Awesome! Now that you've read about some of the amazing archaeological finds in Africa you may want to read about interesting dinosaur finds in Antarctica in the Baby Professor book Paleontology for Kids – Antarctica – Dig Sites and Discoveries.

Visit

BABY PROFESSOR
EDUCATION KIDS

www.BabyProfessorBooks.com

to download Free Baby Professor eBooks
and view our catalog of new and exciting
Children's Books